BROADWAY FAVORITES

Solos and Band Arrangements
Correlated with Essential Elements Band Method

Arranged by
MICHAEL SWEENEY

Welcome to Essential Elements Broadway Favorites! There are two versions of each selection in this versatile book. The SOLO version appears in the beginning of each student book. The FULL BAND arrangements of each song follows. The supplemental CD recording or PIANO ACCOMPANIMENT BOOK may be used as an accompaniment for solo performance. Use these recordings when playing solos for friends and family.

Solo Page	Band Arr. Page	Title	Correlated with Essential Elements
2	13	Beauty And The Beast	Book 1, page 19
3	14	Tomorrow	Book 1, page 19
4	15	Cabaret	Book 1, page 29
5	16	Edelweiss	Book 1, page 29
6	17	Don't Cry For Me Argentina	Book 2, page 14
7	18	Get Me To The Church On Time	Book 2, page 14
8	19	I Dreamed A Dream	Book 2, page 14
9	20	Go Go Go Joseph	Book 2, page 29
10	21	Memory	Book 2, page 29
11	22	The Phantom Of The Opera	Book 2, page 29
12	23	Seventy Six Trombones	Book 2, page 29

ISBN 978-0-7935-9841-0

HAL•LEONARD®
CORPORATION
7777 W. BLUEMOUND RD. P.O. BOX 13819 MILWAUKEE, WI 53213

00860035

2

BEAUTY AND THE BEAST

FLUTE
Solo

Lyrics by HOWARD ASHMAN
Music by ALAN MENKEN
Arranged by MICHAEL SWEENEY

00860035

From the Musical Production ANNIE

TOMORROW

3

FLUTE
Solo

Lyric by MARTIN CHARNIN
Music by CHARLES STROUSE
Arranged by MICHAEL SWEENEY

00860035

From the Musical CABARET
CABARET

FLUTE
Solo

Words by FRED EBB
Music by JOHN KANDER
Arranged by MICHAEL SWEENEY

00860035

EDELWEISS

FLUTE
Solo

Lyrics by OSCAR HAMMERSTEIN II
Music by RICHARD RODGERS
Arranged by MICHAEL SWEENEY

00860035

From EVITA
DON'T CRY FOR ME ARGENTINA

Words by TIM RICE
Music by ANDREW LLOYD WEBBER
Arranged by MICHAEL SWEENEY

FLUTE
Solo

Moderately

mf

13

20

mf

28

35

f

43

mf

51 Maestoso

rit. *f*

57

mf

00860035

MCA Music Publishing

GET ME TO THE CHURCH ON TIME

FLUTE
Solo

Words by ALAN JAY LERNER
Music by FREDERICK LOEWE
Arranged by MICHAEL SWEENEY

00860035

From LES MISÉRABLES
I DREAMED A DREAM

Music by CLAUDE-MICHEL SCHÖNBERG
Lyrics by ALAIN BOUBLIL,
JEAN-MARC NATEL and HERBERT KRETZMER
Arranged by MICHAEL SWEENEY

FLUTE
Solo

From JOSEPH AND THE AMAZING TECHNICOLOR DREAMCOAT
GO GO GO JOSEPH

FLUTE
Solo

Music by ANDREW LLOYD WEBBER
Lyrics by TIM RICE
Arranged by MICHAEL SWEENEY

From CATS
MEMORY

FLUTE
Solo

Music by ANDREW LLOYD WEBBER
Text by TREVOR NUNN after T.S. ELIOT
Arranged by MICHAEL SWEENEY

From THE PHANTOM OF THE OPERA

THE PHANTOM OF THE OPERA

FLUTE
Solo

Music by ANDREW LLOYD WEBBER
Lyrics by CHARLES HART
Additional Lyrics by RICHARD STILGOE and MIKE BATT
Arranged by MICHAEL SWEENEY

From Meredith Willson's THE MUSIC MAN

SEVENTY SIX TROMBONES

By MEREDITH WILLSON
Arranged by MICHAEL SWEENEY

FLUTE
Solo

00860035

From Walt Disney's BEAUTY AND THE BEAST: THE BROADWAY MUSICAL

BEAUTY AND THE BEAST

FLUTE
Band Arrangement

Lyrics by HOWARD ASHMAN
Music by ALAN MENKEN
Arranged by MICHAEL SWEENEY

14

From the Musical Production ANNIE
TOMORROW

FLUTE
Band Arrangement

Lyric by MARTIN CHARNIN
Music by CHARLES STROUSE
Arranged by MICHAEL SWEENEY

From the Musical CABARET
CABARET

FLUTE
Band Arrangement

Words by FRED EBB
Music by JOHN KANDER
Arranged by MICHAEL SWEENEY

From THE SOUND OF MUSIC
EDELWEISS

FLUTE
Band Arrangement

Lyrics by OSCAR HAMMERSTEIN II
Music by RICHARD RODGERS
Arranged by MICHAEL SWEENEY

From EVITA
DON'T CRY FOR ME ARGENTINA

FLUTE
Band Arrangement

Words by TIM RICE
Music by ANDREW LLOYD WEBBER
Arranged by MICHAEL SWEENEY

From MY FAIR LADY
GET ME TO THE CHURCH ON TIME

FLUTE
Band Arrangement

Words by ALAN JAY LERNER
Music by FREDERICK LOEWE
Arranged by MICHAEL SWEENEY

I DREAMED A DREAM

FLUTE
Band Arrangement

Music by CLAUDE-MICHEL SCHÖNBERG
Lyrics by ALAIN BOUBLIL,
JEAN-MARC NATEL and HERBERT KRETZMER
Arranged by MICHAEL SWEENEY

00860035

From JOSEPH AND THE AMAZING TECHNICOLOR DREAMCOAT
GO GO GO JOSEPH

FLUTE
Band Arrangement

Music by ANDREW LLOYD WEBBER
Lyrics by TIM RICE
Arranged by MICHAEL SWEENEY

From CATS
MEMORY

FLUTE
Band Arrangement

Music by ANDREW LLOYD WEBBER
Text by TREVOR NUNN after T.S. ELIOT
Arranged by MICHAEL SWEENEY

From THE PHANTOM OF THE OPERA

THE PHANTOM OF THE OPERA

FLUTE
Band Arrangement

Music by ANDREW LLOYD WEBBER
Lyrics by CHARLES HART
Additional Lyrics by RICHARD STILGOE and MIKE BATT
Arranged by MICHAEL SWEENEY

From Meredith Willson's THE MUSIC MAN

SEVENTY SIX TROMBONES

FLUTE
Band Arrangement

By MEREDITH WILLSON
Arranged by MICHAEL SWEENEY